LISTEN, CHILDREN, LISTEN

also by Myra Cohn Livingston

WHISPERS and Other Poems

WIDE AWAKE and Other Poems

I'M HIDING

SEE WHAT I FOUND

I TALK TO ELEPHANTS!

I'M NOT ME

HAPPY BIRTHDAY

THE MOON AND A STAR and Other Poems

I'M WAITING

OLD MRS. TWINDLYTART and Other Rhymes

A CRAZY FLIGHT and Other Poems

also edited by Myra Cohn Livingston

A TUNE BEYOND US: A Collection of Poetry

SPEAK ROUGHLY TO YOUR LITTLE BOY:
    A Collection of Parodies and Burlesques, Together with
    the Original Poems, Chosen and Annotated for Young People

Listen, Children, Listen

An Anthology of Poems for
the Very Young

Edited by
Myra Cohn Livingston

Illustrated by Trina Schart Hyman

Harcourt Brace Jovanovich, Inc., New York

To Carter, Jennifer and Kristin

Every effort has been made to trace the ownership of all copyrighted material and to secure the necessary permissions to reprint these selections. In the event of any question arising as to
the use of any material, the editor and the publisher, while ex-
pressing regret for any inadvertent error, will be happy to make
the necessary correction in future printings. Thanks are due to
the following for permission to reprint the copyrighted material
listed below:
GEORGE ALLEN & UNWIN LTD. for ''Oliphaunt'' from *The Adven-
tures of Tom Bombadil* by Professor J. R. R. Tolkien.
ATHENEUM PUBLISHERS for ''I Did Not See a Mermaid'' from
Feather in My Hand by Siddie Joe Johnson, text copyright ©
1967 by Siddie Joe Johnson.
J. M. DENT & SONS LTD. and the TRUSTEES FOR THE COPYRIGHTS
OF THE LATE DYLAN THOMAS for ''Johnnie Crack and Flossie
Snail'' from *Under Milkwood* by Dylan Thomas.
DODD, MEAD & COMPANY, INC., for ''Calico Pie,'' ''There was an
old lady of France,'' ''There was an old man on the Border,''

LISTEN, CHILDREN, LISTEN

A CRADLE SONG

by William Butler Yeats

The angels are stooping
Above your bed;
They weary of trooping
With the whimpering dead.

God's laughing in Heaven
To see you so good;
The Sailing Seven
Are gay with His mood.

I sigh that kiss you,
For I must own
That I shall miss you
When you have grown.

THE LAMB

by Theodore Roethke

The Lamb just says, I AM!
He frisks and whisks, *He* can.
He jumps all over. Who
Are *you?* You're jumping too!

LITTLE BUSH

A SONG

by Elizabeth Madox Roberts

A little bush
At the picnic place,
A little bush could talk to me.

I ran away
And hid myself,
And I found a bush that could talk to me,
A smooth little bush said a word to me.

A SMALL DISCOVERY

by James A. Emanuel

Father,
Where do giants go to cry?

To the hills
Behind the thunder?
Or to the waterfall?
I wonder.

(Giants cry.
I know they do.
Do they wait
Till nighttime too?)

SOLITUDE

by A. A. Milne

I have a house where I go
   When there's too many people,
I have a house where I go
   Where no one can be;
I have a house where I go,
Where nobody ever says "No";
Where no one says anything—so
   There is no one but me.

I NEVER SAW A MOOR

by Emily Dickinson

I never saw a moor,
I never saw the sea;
Yet know I how the heather looks,
And what a wave must be.

I never spoke with God,
Nor visited in heaven;
Yet certain am I of the spot
As if the chart were given.

THE YAK

by Theodore Roethke

There was a most odious Yak
Who took only toads on his Back:
If you asked for a Ride,
He would act very Snide,
And go humping off, yicketty-yak.

BLUM

by Dorothy Aldis

Dog means dog,
And cat means cat;
And there are lots
Of words like that.

A cart's a cart
To pull or shove,
A plate's a plate
To eat off of.

But there are other
Words I say
When I am left
Alone to play.

Blum is one.
Blum is a word
That very few
Have ever heard.

I like to say it,
"Blum, Blum, Blum"—
I do it loud
Or in a hum.

All by itself
It's nice to sing:
It does not mean
A single thing.

NUMBERS

by Elizabeth Madox Roberts

When I can count the numbers far,
And know all the figures that there are,

Then I'll know everything, and I
Can know about the ground and sky,

And all the little bugs I see,
And I'll count the leaves on the silver-leaf tree,
And all the days that ever can be.

I'll know all the cows and sheep that pass,
And I'll know all the grass,

And all the places far away,
And I'll know everything some day.

WHISPERS

by Myra Cohn Livingston

Whispers
     tickle through your ear
     telling things you like to hear.

Whispers
     are as soft as skin
     letting little words curl in.

Whispers
     come so they can blow
     secrets others never know.

THE SWING

by Robert Louis Stevenson

How do you like to go up in a swing,
    Up in the air so blue?
Oh, I do think it the pleasantest thing
    Ever a child can do!

Up in the air and over the wall,
    Till I can see so wide,
Rivers and trees and cattle and all
    Over the countryside—

Till I look down on the garden green,
    Down on the roof so brown—
Up in the air I go flying again,
    Up in the air and down!

by e. e. cummings

who are you, little i

(five or six years old)
peering from some high

window; at the gold

of november sunset

(and feeling: that if day
has to become night

this is a beautiful way)

TRIOLET

by G. K. Chesterton

I wish I were a jelly fish
That cannot fall downstairs:
Of all the things I wish to wish
I wish I were a jelly fish
That hasn't any cares,
And doesn't even have to wish
"I wish I were a jelly fish
That cannot fall downstairs."

DISCOVERY

by Myra Cohn Livingston

Round and round and round I spin
Making a circle so I can fall in.

TO A SQUIRREL AT KYLE-NA-NO

by William Butler Yeats

Come play with me;
Why should you run
Through the shaking tree
As though I'd a gun
To strike you dead?
When all I would do
Is to scratch your head
And let you go.

THE LITTLE TURTLE

by Vachel Lindsay

There was a little turtle.
He lived in a box.
He swam in a puddle.
He climbed on the rocks.

He snapped at a mosquito.
He snapped at a flea.
He snapped at a minnow.
And he snapped at me.

He caught the mosquito.
He caught the flea.
He caught the minnow.
But he didn't catch me.

HOW DOTH THE LITTLE CROCODILE

by Lewis Carroll

How doth the little crocodile
   Improve his shining tail,
And pour the waters of the Nile
   On every golden scale!

How cheerfully he seems to grin,
   How neatly spreads his claws,
And welcomes little fishes in,
   With gently smiling jaws!

FIREFLY

A SONG

by Elizabeth Madox Roberts

A little light is going by,
Is going up to see the sky,
A little light with wings.

I never could have thought of it,
To have a little bug all lit
And made to go on wings.

THE HENS

by Elizabeth Madox Roberts

The night was coming very fast;
It reached the gate as I ran past.

The pigeons had gone to the tower of the church
And all the hens were on their perch,

Up in the barn, and I thought I heard
A piece of a little purring word.

I stopped inside, waiting and staying,
To try to hear what the hens were saying.

They were asking something, that was plain,
Asking it over and over again.

One of them moved and turned around,
Her feathers made a ruffled sound,

A ruffled sound, like a bushful of birds,
And she said her little asking words.

She pushed her head close into her wing,
But nothing answered anything.

THE SONG OF THE JELLICLES

by T. S. Eliot

> *Jellicle Cats come out tonight,*
> *Jellicle Cats come one come all:*
> *The Jellicle Moon is shining bright—*
> *Jellicles come to the Jellicle Ball.*

Jellicle Cats are black and white,
Jellicle Cats are rather small;
Jellicle Cats are merry and bright,
And pleasant to hear when they caterwaul.
Jellicle Cats have cheerful faces,
Jellicle Cats have bright black eyes;
They like to practise their airs and graces
And wait for the Jellicle Moon to rise.

Jellicle Cats develop slowly,
Jellicle Cats are not too big;
Jellicle Cats are roly-poly,
They know how to dance a gavotte and a jig.
Until the Jellicle Moon appears
They make their toilette and take their repose:
Jellicles wash behind their ears,
Jellicles dry between their toes.

Jellicle Cats are white and black,
Jellicle Cats are of moderate size;
Jellicles jump like a jumping-jack,
Jellicle Cats have moonlit eyes.
They're quiet enough in the morning hours,
They're quiet enough in the afternoon,
Reserving their terpsichorean powers
To dance by the light of the Jellicle Moon.

Jellicle Cats are black and white,
Jellicle Cats (as I said) are small;
If it happens to be a stormy night
They will practise a caper or two in the hall.
If it happens the sun is shining bright
You would say they had nothing to do at all:
They are resting and saving themselves to be
    right
For the Jellicle Moon and the Jellicle Ball.

CAT

by Mary Britton Miller

The black cat yawns,
Opens her jaws,
Stretches her legs,
And shows her claws.

Then she gets up
And stands on four
Long stiff legs
And yawns some more.

She shows her sharp teeth,
She stretches her lip,
Her slice of tongue
Turns up at the tip.

Lifting herself
On her delicate toes,
She arches her back
As high as it goes.

She lets herself down
With particular care
And pads away
With her tail in the air.

THE FROG

by Hilaire Belloc

Be kind and tender to the Frog,
   And do not call him names,
As 'Slimy skin,' or 'Polly-wog,'
   Or likewise 'Ugly James,'
Or 'Gap-a-grin,' or 'Toad-gone-wrong,'
   Or 'Bill Bandy-knees':
The Frog is justly sensitive
   To epithets like these.
No animal will more repay
   A treatment kind and fair;
At least so lonely people say
Who keep a frog (and, by the way,
   They are extremely rare).

THE SWALLOWS

by Elizabeth Coatsworth

Nine swallows sat on a telephone wire:
"Teeter, teeter," and then they were still,
all facing one way, with the sun like a fire
along their blue shoulders, and hot on each bill.
But they sat there so quietly, all of the nine,
that I almost forgot they were swallows at all.
They seemed more like clothespins left out on
    the line
when the wash is just dried, and the first rain-
    drops fall.

SNAIL

by John Drinkwater

Snail upon the wall,
Have you got at all
Anything to tell
About your shell?

Only this, my child—
When the wind is wild,
Or when the sun is hot,
It's all I've got.

by *Christina Rossetti*

The horses of the sea
  Rear a foaming crest,
But the horses of the land
  Serve us the best.

The horses of the land
  Munch corn and clover,
While the foaming sea-horses
  Toss and turn over.

OLIPHAUNT

by J. R. R. Tolkien

Grey as a mouse,
Big as a house,
Nose like a snake,
I make the earth shake,
As I tramp through the grass;
Trees crack as I pass.
With horns in my mouth
I walk in the South,
Flapping big ears.
Beyond count of years
I stump round and round,
Never lie on the ground,
Not even to die.
Oliphaunt am I,
Biggest of all,
Huge, old, and tall.
If ever you'd met me,
You wouldn't forget me.
If you never do,
You won't think I'm true;
But old Oliphaunt am I,
And I never lie.

TEA PARTY

by Harry Behn

Mister Beedle Baddlebug,
Don't bandle up in your boodlebag
Or numble in your jimblejug,
Now eat your nummy tiffletag
Or I will never invite you
To tea again with me. Shoo!

CIRCLES

by Harry Behn

The things to draw with compasses
Are suns and moons and circleses
And rows of humptydumpasses
Or anything in circuses
Like hippopotamusseses
And hoops and camels' humpasses
And wheels on clownses busseses
And fat old elephumpasses.

HALFWAY DOWN

by A. A. Milne

Halfway down the stairs
Is a stair
Where I sit.
There isn't any
Other stair
Quite like
It.
I'm not at the bottom,
I'm not at the top;
So this is the stair
Where
I always
Stop.

Halfway up the stairs
Isn't up,
And isn't down.
It isn't in the nursery,
It isn't in the town.
And all sorts of funny thoughts
Run round my head:
"It isn't really
Anywhere!
It's somewhere else
Instead!"

by Christina Rossetti

All the bells were ringing
And all the birds were singing,
When Molly sat down crying
  For her broken doll:
  O you silly Moll!
Sobbing and sighing
  For a broken doll,
When all the bells are ringing
And all the birds are singing.

THE SHELL
by David McCord

I took away the ocean once,
Spiraled in a shell,
And happily for months and months
I heard it very well.

How is it then that I should hear
What months and months before
Had blown upon me sad and clear,
Down by the grainy shore?

SEA SHELL

by Amy Lowell

Sea Shell, Sea Shell,
  Sing me a song, O Please!
A song of ships, and sailor men,
  And parrots, and tropical trees,

Of islands lost in the Spanish Main
Which no man ever may find again,
Of fishes and corals under the waves,
And seahorses stabled in great green caves.

Sea Shell, Sea Shell,
Sing of the things you know so well.

THE CEILING

by Theodore Roethke

Suppose the Ceiling went Outside
And then caught Cold and Up and Died?
The only Thing we'd have for Proof
That he was Gone, would be the Roof;
I think it would be Most Revealing
To find out how the Ceiling's Feeling.

CITY

by Langston Hughes

In the morning the city
Spreads its wings
Making a song
In stone that sings.

In the evening the city
Goes to bed
Hanging lights
About its head.

BABY TOES

by Carl Sandburg

There is a blue star, Janet,
Fifteen years' ride from us,
If we ride a hundred miles an hour.

There is a white star, Janet,
Forty years' ride from us,
If we ride a hundred miles an hour.

       Shall we ride
       To the blue star
       Or the white star?

JOHNNIE CRACK AND FLOSSIE SNAIL

from UNDER MILKWOOD

by Dylan Thomas

Johnnie Crack and Flossie Snail
Kept their baby in a milking pail
Flossie Snail and Johnnie Crack
One would pull it out and one would put it back

O it's my turn now said Flossie Snail
To take the baby from the milking pail
And it's my turn now said Johnnie Crack
To smack it on the head and put it back

Johnnie Crack and Flossie Snail
Kept their baby in a milking pail
One would put it back and one would pull it out
And all it had to drink was ale and stout
For Johnnie Crack and Flossie Snail
Always used to say that stout and ale
Was *good* for a baby in a milking pail.

BUNCHES OF GRAPES

by Walter de la Mare

"Bunches of grapes," says Timothy;
"Pomegranates pink," says Elaine;
"A junket of cream and a cranberry tart
    For me," says Jane.

"Love-in-a-mist," says Timothy;
"Primroses pale," says Elaine;
"A nosegay of pinks and mignonette
    For me," says Jane.

"Chariots of gold," says Timothy;
"Silvery wings," says Elaine;
"A bumpity ride in a wagon of hay
    For me," says Jane.

by Christina Rossetti

Mix a pancake,
Stir a pancake,
   Pop it in the pan;
Fry the pancake,
Toss the pancake,—
   Catch it if you can.

from DREAM-PEDLARY

by Thomas Lovell Beddoes

I

If there were dreams to sell,
    What would you buy?
Some cost a passing bell;
    Some a light sigh,
That shakes from Life's fresh crown
Only a roseleaf down.
If there were dreams to sell,
Merry and sad to tell,
And the crier rung the bell,
    What would you buy?

BOBBILY BOO AND WOLLYPOTUMP

by Laura E. Richards

Bobbily Boo, the king so free,
He used to drink the Mango tea.
Mango tea and coffee, too,
He drank them both till his nose turned blue.

Wollypotump, the queen so high,
She used to eat the Gumbo pie.
Gumbo pie and Gumbo cake,
She ate them both till her teeth did break.

Bobbily Boo and Wollypotump,
Each called the other a greedy frump.
And when these terrible words were said,
They sat and cried till they both were dead.

by Edward Lear

There was an old man on the Border,
Who lived in the utmost disorder;
He danced with the cat, and made tea in his hat,
Which vexed all the folks on the Border.

There was an old person of Ware,
Who rode on the back of a bear:
When they ask'd, "Does it trot?"
       he said, "Certainly not!
He's a Moppsikon Floppsikon bear!"

There was an old lady of France,
Who taught little ducklings to dance;
When she said, "Tick-a-tack!" they only said,
       "Quack!"
Which grieved that old lady of France.

THE NEW LITTLE BOY

by Harry Behn

A new little boy moved in next door
So I climbed a tree and bounced on a limb
And asked where he used to live before
And he didn't know but his name was Tim,
So I told all three of my names to him.

When he didn't say anything after that
I hung by my knees to see if he scared
And meowed and made my face like a cat,
But he only stood in his yard and stared,
He only watched like he never cared.

Well, all I know is his name is Tim
And I don't think very much of him.

TIRED TIM

by Walter de la Mare

Poor tired Tim! It's sad for him.
He lags the long bright morning through,
Ever so tired of nothing to do;
He moons and mopes the livelong day,
Nothing to think about, nothing to say;

Up to bed with his candle to creep,
Too tired to yawn, too tired to sleep:
Poor tired Tim! It's sad for him.

SOME ONE

by Walter de la Mare

Some one came knocking
    At my wee, small door;
Some one came knocking,
    I'm sure—sure—sure;
I listened, I opened,
    I looked to left and right,
But nought there was a-stirring
    In the still dark night;
Only the busy beetle
    Tap-tapping in the wall,
Only from the forest
    The screech-owl's call,
Only the cricket whistling
    While the dewdrops fall,
So I know not who came knocking,
    At all, at all, at all.

OVERHEARD ON A SALTMARSH

by Harold Monro

Nymph, nymph, what are your beads?

Green glass, goblin. Why do you stare at them?

Give them me.

        No.

Give them me. Give them me.

            No.

Then I will howl all night in the reeds,
Lie in the mud and howl for them.

Goblin, why do you love them so?

They are better than stars or water,
Better than voices of winds that sing,
Better than any man's fair daughter,
Your green glass beads on a silver ring.

Hush, I stole them out of the moon.

Give me your beads, I want them.

           No.

I will howl in a deep lagoon
For your green glass beads. I love them so.
Give them me. Give them.

             No.

from THE MERMAID
by Alfred, Lord Tennyson

I

Who would be
A mermaid fair,
Singing alone,
Combing her hair
Under the sea,
In a golden curl
With a comb of pearl,
On a throne?

II

I would be a mermaid fair;
I would sing to myself the whole of the day;
With a comb of pearl I would comb my hair;
And still as I comb'd I would sing and say,
"Who is it loves me? Who loves not me?"
I would comb my hair till my ringlets would fall
　　Low adown, low adown.
From under my starry sea-bud crown
　　Low adown and around,
And I should look like a fountain of gold

Springing alone
With a shrill inner sound,
Over the throne
In the midst of the hall; . . .

THE LAST WORD OF A BLUEBIRD

As Told to a Child

by Robert Frost

As I went out a Crow
In a low voice said, ''Oh,
I was looking for you.
How do you do?
I just came to tell you
To tell Lesley (will you?)
That her little Bluebird
Wanted me to bring word
That the north wind last night
That made the stars bright
And made ice on the trough
Almost made him cough
His tail feathers off.
He just had to fly!
But he sent her Good-by,
And said to be good,
And wear her red hood,
And look for skunk tracks
In the snow with an ax—
And do everything!
And perhaps in the spring
He would come back and sing.''

NEAR AND FAR

by Harry Behn

What do hens say
With all their talking?
What luck! What luck! they cluck,
Look, look! they say
As they settle
In a sunny nook
And scoop
Dust under their feathers.

What does the ditch digging machine
Chatter about
Scratching
Into the dirt?
Who do I thank
For these scrumptious
Scrunchy
Chunks of rock? it asks
With a clatter and clank
As it stacks the cool earth up
In a neat brown bank.

Only in summer
The big machine
And loose old hens
Play the same scooping
Sunny game,
Saying the same things over and over
At about the same loudness
Because the machine is farther away.

BOBADIL

by James Reeves

Far from far
  Lives Bobadil
In a tall house
  On a tall hill.

Out from the high
  Top window-sill
On a clear night
  Leans Bobadil

To touch the moon,
  To catch a star,
To keep in her tall house
  Far from far.

THE HILLS

by Rachel Field

Sometimes I think the hills
That loom across the harbor
Lie there like sleeping dragons,
Crouched one above another,
With trees for tufts of fur
Growing all up and down
The ridges and humps of their backs,
And orange cliffs for claws
Dipped in the sea below.
Sometimes a wisp of smoke
Rises out of the hollows,
As if in their dragon sleep
They dreamed of strange old battles.

What if the hills should stir
Some day and stretch themselves,
Shake off the clinging trees
And all the clustered houses?

OLD SHELLOVER

by Walter de la Mare

"Come!" said Old Shellover.
"What?" says Creep.
"The horny old Gardener's fast asleep;
The fat cock Thrush
To his nest has gone,
And the dew shines bright
In the rising Moon;
Old Sallie Worm from her hole doth peep;
"Come!" said Old Shellover.
"Aye!" said Creep.

I DID NOT SEE A MERMAID?

by Siddie Joe Johnson

I did not see a mermaid
The day I looked for one.
Perhaps the sun was in my eyes—
There was a lot of sun.

Just as the teardrops started down
My disappointed face,
I blinked my eyes to stop them
And I looked away in space;

I looked away in space and saw,
Almost far out at sea,
A porpoise and a Something—
And the porpoise winked at me.

THE MOON'S THE NORTH WIND'S COOKY
(What the little girl said)

by Vachel Lindsay

The Moon's the North Wind's cooky.
He bites it, day by day,
Until there's but a rim of scraps
That crumble all away.

The South Wind is a baker.
He kneads clouds in his den,
And bakes a crisp new moon *that . . . greedy*
North . . . Wind . . . eats . . . again!

THE FAIRIES

by William Allingham

Up the airy mountain,
  Down the rushy glen,
We daren't go a-hunting
  For fear of little men;
Wee folk, good folk,
  Trooping all together;
Green jacket, red cap,
  And white owl's feather!

Down along the rocky shore
  Some make their home,
They live on crispy pancakes
  Of yellow tide-foam;
Some in the reeds
  Of the black mountain lake,
With frogs for their watch-dogs,
  All night awake.

High on the hill-top
  The old King sits;
He is now so old and gray,
  He's nigh lost his wits.
With a bridge of white mist

Columbkill he crosses,
On his stately journeys
    From Slieveleague to Rosses;
Or going up with music
    On cold starry nights,
To sup with the Queen
    Of the gay Northern Lights.

They stole little Bridget
    For seven years long;
When she came down again
    Her friends were all gone.
They took her lightly back,
    Between the night and morrow,
They thought that she was fast asleep,
    But she was dead with sorrow.
They have kept her ever since
    Deep within the lake,
On a bed of flag-leaves,
    Watching till she wake.

By the craggy hill-side,
    Through the mosses bare,
They have planted thorn-trees
    For pleasure here and there.
Is any man so daring
    As dig them up in spite,
He shall find their sharpest thorns
    In his bed at night.

WHERE THE BEE SUCKS
from THE TEMPEST

by William Shakespeare

Where the bee sucks, there suck I.
In a cowslip's bell I lie,
There I couch when owls do cry.
On the bat's back I do fly
After summer merrily.
Merrily, merrily shall I live now
Under the blossom that hangs on the bough.

Up the airy mountain,
   Down the rushy glen,
We daren't go a-hunting
   For fear of little men;
Wee folk, good folk,
   Trooping all together;
Green jacket, red cap,
   And white owl's feather!

CALICO PIE

by Edward Lear

I

Calico pie,
The little birds fly
Down to the calico-tree:
   Their wings were blue,
   And they sang "Tilly-loo!"
   Till away they flew;
And they never came back to me!
   They never came back,
   They never came back,
They never came back to me!

II

Calico jam,
The little Fish swam
Over the Syllabub Sea.
   He took off his hat
   To the Sole and the Sprat,
   And the Willeby-wat:
But he never came back to me;
   He never came back,
   He never came back,
He never came back to me.

III

Calico ban,
The little Mice ran
To be ready in time for tea;
Flippity flup,
They drank it all up,
And danced in the cup:
But they never came back to me;
They never came back,
They never came back,
They never came back to me.

IV

Calico drum,
The Grasshoppers come,
The Butterfly, Beetle, and Bee,
Over the ground,
Around and round,
With a hop and a bound;
But they never came back,
They never came back,
They never came back,
They never came back to me.

POTOMAC TOWN IN FEBRUARY

by Carl Sandburg

The bridge says: Come across, try me; see how
    good I am.
The big rock in the river says: Look at me;
    learn how to stand up.
The white water says: I go on; around, under,
    over, I go on.
A kneeling, scraggly pine says: I am here yet;
    they nearly got me last year.
A sliver of moon slides by on a high wind calling:
    I know why; I'll see you tomorrow; I'll tell
    you everything tomorrow.

SPRING

by William Blake

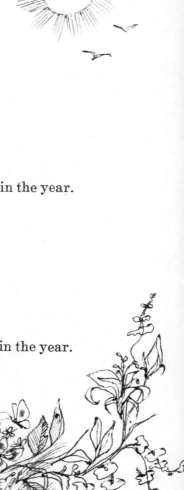

Sound the flute!
Now it's mute.
Birds delight
Day and night;
Nightingale
In the dale,
Lark in sky,
Merrily,
Merrily, merrily, to welcome in the year.

Little boy,
Full of joy;
Little girl,
Sweet and small;
Cock does crow,
So do you;
Merry voice,
Infant noise,
Merrily, merrily, to welcome in the year.

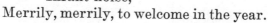

Little lamb,
Here I am;
Come and lick
My white neck;
Let me pull
Your soft wool;
Let me kiss
Your soft face;
Merrily, merrily, we welcome in the year.

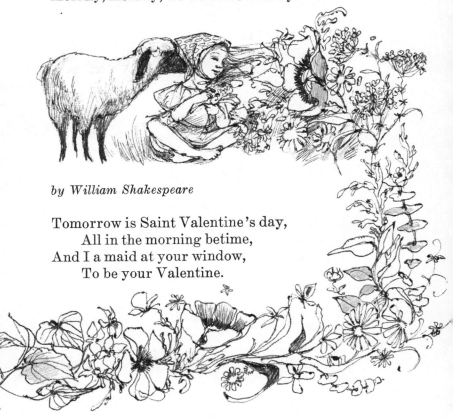

by William Shakespeare

Tomorrow is Saint Valentine's day,
    All in the morning betime,
And I a maid at your window,
    To be your Valentine.

PIPPA'S SONG

by Robert Browning

The year's at the spring,
And day's at the morn;
Morning's at seven;
The hillside's dew-pearled;
The lark's on the wing;
The snail's on the thorn;
God's in His heaven—
All's right with the world.

APRIL RAIN SONG

by Langston Hughes

Let the rain kiss you.
Let the rain beat upon your head with silver
    liquid drops.
Let the rain sing you a lullaby.

The rain makes still pools on the sidewalk.
The rain makes running pools in the gutter.
The rain plays a little sleep-song on our roof at
    night—

And I love the rain.

WHERE GO THE BOATS?

by Robert Louis Stevenson

Dark brown is the river,
   Golden is the sand.
It flows along forever,
   With trees on either hand.

Green leaves a-floating,
   Castles of the foam,
Boats of mine a-boating—
   Where will all come home?

On goes the river
   And out past the mill,
Away down the valley,
   Away down the hill.

Away down the river,
   A hundred miles or more,
Other little children
   Shall bring my boats ashore.

THE PASTURE

by Robert Frost

I'm going out to clean the pasture spring;
I'll only stop to rake the leaves away
(And wait to watch the water clear, I may):
I sha'n't be gone long.—You come too.

I'm going out to fetch the little calf
That's standing by the mother. It's so young
It totters when she licks it with her tongue.
I sha'n't be gone long.—You come too.

THE SUN

by John Drinkwater

I told the Sun that I was glad,
 I'm sure I don't know why;
Somehow the pleasant way he had
 Of shining in the sky,
Just put a notion in my head
 That wouldn't it be fun
If, walking on the hill, I said
 "I'm happy" to the Sun.

AT THE SEASIDE

by Robert Louis Stevenson

When I was down beside the sea
A wooden spade they gave to me
 To dig the sandy shore.
My holes were empty like a cup,
In every hole the sea came up,
 Till it could come no more.

THEME IN YELLOW

by Carl Sandburg

I spot the hills
With yellow balls in autumn.
I light the prairie cornfields
Orange and tawny gold clusters
And I am called pumpkins.
On the last of October
When dusk is fallen
Children join hands
And circle round me
Singing ghost songs
And love to the harvest moon;
I am a jack-o'-lantern
With terrible teeth
And the children know
I am fooling.

WHO HAS SEEN THE WIND?

by Christina Rossetti

Who has seen the wind?
   Neither I nor you:
But when the leaves hang trembling
   The wind is passing thro'.

Who has seen the wind?
   Neither you nor I:
But when the trees bow down their heads
   The wind is passing by.

CYNTHIA IN THE SNOW

by Gwendolyn Brooks

IT SUSHES.
It hushes
The loudness in the road.
It flitter-twitters,
And laughs away from me.
It laughs a lovely whiteness,
And whitely whirs away,
To be
Some otherwhere,
Still white as milk or shirts.
So beautiful it hurts.

from THE WIND AND THE MOON

by George MacDonald

Said the Wind to the Moon, "I will blow you out;
     You stare
     In the air
     Like a ghost in a chair,
Always looking what I am about—
I hate to be watched; I'll blow you out."

THE SNOWFLAKE

by Walter de la Mare

Before I melt,
Come, look at me!
This lovely icy filigree!
Of a great forest
In one night
I make a wilderness
Of white:
By skyey cold
Of crystals made,
All softly, on
Your finger laid,
I pause, that you
My beauty see:
Breathe, and I vanish
Instantly.

I HEARD A BIRD SING

by Oliver Herford

I heard a bird sing
　In the dark of December
A magical thing
　And sweet to remember.
"We are nearer to Spring
　Than we were in September,"
I heard a bird sing
　In the dark of December.

from HESPERUS

by James Stephens

Evening gathers everything
Scattered by the morning!

Fold for sheep, and nest for wing;
Evening gathers everything!

Child to mother, queen to king,
Running at thy warning!

Evening gathers everything
Scattered by the morning!

THE LAMB

by William Blake

Little Lamb, who made thee?
Dost thou know who made thee?
Gave thee life, and bid thee feed,
By the stream and o'er the mead;
Gave thee clothing of delight,
Softest clothing, wooly, bright;
Gave thee such a tender voice,
Making all the vales rejoice?
Little Lamb, who made thee?
Dost thou know who made thee?

Little Lamb, I'll tell thee,
Little Lamb, I'll tell thee:
He is called by thy name,
For He calls Himself a Lamb.
He is meek, and He is mild;
He became a little child.
I a child, and thou a lamb,
We are called by His name.
Little Lamb, God bless thee!
Little Lamb, God bless thee!

by e. e. cummings

little tree
little silent Christmas tree
you are so little
you are more like a flower

who found you in the green forest
and were you very sorry to come away?
see   i will comfort you
because you smell so sweetly

i will kiss your cool bark
and hug you safe and tight
just as your mother would,
only don't be afraid

look   the spangles
that sleep all the year in a dark box
dreaming of being taken out and allowed to
      shine,
the balls the chains red and gold the fluffy
      threads,

put up your little arms
and i'll give them all to you to hold
every finger shall have its ring
and there won't be a single place dark or
      unhappy

then when you're quite dressed
you'll stand in the window for everyone to see
and how they'll stare!
oh but you'll be very proud

and my little sister and i will take hands
and looking up at our beautiful tree
we'll dance and sing
"Noel Noel"

IN THE WEEK WHEN
CHRISTMAS COMES

by Eleanor Farjeon

This is the week when Christmas comes.

Let every pudding burst with plums,
And every tree bear dolls and drums,
  In the week when Christmas comes.

Let every hall have boughs of green,
With berries glowing in between,
  In the week when Christmas comes.

Let every doorstep have a song
Sounding the dark street along,
  In the week when Christmas comes.

Let every steeple ring a bell
With a joyful tale to tell,
  In the week when Christmas comes.

Let every night put forth a star
To show us where the heavens are,
  In the week when Christmas comes.

Let every stable have a lamb
Sleeping warm beside its dam
  In the week when Christmas comes.

This is the week when Christmas comes.

CAROL OF THE BROWN KING

by Langston Hughes

Of the three Wise Men
Who came to the King,
One was a brown man,
So they sing.

Of the three Wise Men
Who followed the Star,
One was a brown king
From afar.

They brought fine gifts
Of spices and gold
In jeweled boxes
Of beauty untold.

Unto His humble
Manger they came
And bowed their heads
In Jesus' name.

Three Wise Men,
One dark like me—
Part of His
Nativity.

by Christina Rossetti

What can I give Him,
  Poor as I am?
If I were a shepherd
  I would bring a lamb,
If I were a Wise Man
  I would do my part,—
Yet what I can I give Him,
  Give my heart.

THE PIPER

by William Blake

Piping down the valleys wild,
   Piping songs of pleasant glee,
On a cloud I saw a child,
   And he laughing said to me:

"Pipe a song about a lamb!"
   So I piped with merry cheer.
"Piper, pipe that song again";
   So I piped: he wept to hear.

"Drop thy pipe, thy happy pipe;
   Sing thy songs of happy cheer!"
So I sung the same again,
   While he wept with joy to hear.

"Piper, sit thee down and write
   In a book that all may read."
So he vanished from my sight;
   And I plucked a hollow reed,

And I made a rural pen,
   And I stained the water clear,
And I wrote my happy songs
   Every child may joy to hear.

WHO CALLS?

by Frances Clarke Sayers

"Listen, children, listen, won't you come into
   the night?
The stars have set their candle gleam, the moon
   her lanthorn light.
I'm piping little tunes for you to catch your
   dancing feet.
There's glory in the heavens, but there's magic
   in the street.
There's jesting here and carnival: the cost of
   a balloon
Is an ancient rhyme said backwards, and a
   wish upon the moon.
The city walls and city streets!—you shall make
   of these
As fair a thing as country roads and blossomy
   apple trees."

"What watchman calls us in the night, and
   plays a little tune
That turns our tongues to talking now of April,
   May and June?
Who bids us come with nimble feet and snap-
   ping finger tips?"
"I am the Spring, the Spring, the Spring with
   laughter on my lips."

Index of Poems

Index of Authors